Garbage

Also by A. R. Ammons

Ommateum

Expressions of Sea Level

Corsons Inlet

Tape for the Turn of the Year

Northfield Poems

Selected Poems

Uplands

Briefings

Collected Poems: 1951–1971
(winner of the National Book Award for Poetry, 1973)

Sphere: The Form of a Motion
(winner of the 1973–1974 Bollingen Prize in Poetry)

Diversifications

The Snow Poems

Highgate Road

The Selected Poems: 1951–1977

Selected Longer Poems

A Coast of Trees
(winner of the National Book Critics Circle Award for Poetry, 1981)

Worldly Hopes

Lake Effect Country

The Selected Poems: Expanded Edition

Sumerian Vistas

The Really Short Poems

Garbage

A . R . Ammons

W.W. Norton

& Company

New York

London

Copyright © 1993 by A. R. Ammons

Printed in the United States of America

The text of this book is composed in 10.5/13.5 Janson
with the display set in Centaur Monotype Bold at 70% horizontal scale
Composed by PennSet, Inc.
Manufacturing by Courier Companies, Inc.
Book design by Margaret M. Wagner

Library of Congress Cataloging-in-Publication Data
Ammons, A. R., 1926–
Garbage / by A. R. Ammons.
p.   cm.
I. Title.
PS3501.M6G37   1993
811'.54—dc20   92-42490

ISBN 0-393-03542-5

W. W. Norton & Company, Inc., 500 Fifth Avenue, New York, NY 10110
W. W. Norton & Company Ltd., 10 Coptic Street, London WC1A 1PU

2 3 4 5 6 7 8 9 0

*to the bacteria, tumblebugs, scavengers,
wordsmiths—the transfigurers, restorers*

Parts 1 through 5 appeared under the title "Garbage" in *The American Poetry Review*, March/April 1992.

Part 6 appeared under the title "Radiant Days" in *CrossRoads*, Fall 1992.

Part 11 appeared under the title "Going Places" in *Pearl*, December 1992.

My thanks to those assisting in these appearances.

Garbage

Creepy little creepers are insinuatingly
curling up my spine (bringing the message)

saying, Boy!, are you writing that great poem
the world's waiting for: don't you know you

have an unaccomplished mission unaccomplished;
someone somewhere may be at this very moment

dying for the lack of what W. C. Williams says
you could (or somebody could) be giving: yeah?

so, these little messengers say, what do you
mean teaching school (teaching *poetry* and

poetry writing and wasting your time painting
sober little organic, meaningful pictures)

when values thought lost (but only scrambled into
disengagement) lie around demolished

and centerless because you (that's me, boy)
haven't elaborated everything in everybody's

face, yet: on the other hand (I say to myself,
receiving the messengers and cutting them down)

who has done anything or am I likely to do
anything the world won't twirl without: and

since SS's enough money (I hope) to live
from now on on in elegance and simplicity—

or, maybe, just simplicity—why shouldn't I
at my age (63) concentrate on chucking the

advancements and rehearsing the sweetnesses of
leisure, nonchalance, and small-time byways: couple

months ago, for example, I went all the way
from soy flakes (already roasted and pressed

and in need of an hour's simmering boil
to be cooked) all the way to soybeans, the

pure golden pearls themselves, 65¢ lb. dry: they
have to be soaked overnight in water and they

have to be boiled slowly for six hours—but
they're welfare cheap, are a complete protein,

more protein by weight than meat, more
calcium than milk, more lecithin than eggs,

and somewhere in there the oil that smoothes
stools, a great virtue: I need time and verve

to find out, now, about medicare/medicaid,
national osteoporosis week, gadabout tours,

hearing loss, homesharing programs, and choosing
good nutrition! for starters! why should I

be trying to write my flattest poem, now, for
whom, not for myself, for others?, posh, as I

have never said: Social Security can provide
the beans, soys enough: my house, paid for for

twenty years, is paid for: my young'un
is raised: nothing one can pay cash for seems

very valuable: that reaches a high enough
benchmark for me—high enough that I wouldn't

know what to do with anything beyond that, no
place to house it, park it, dock it, let it drift

down to: elegance and simplicity: I wonder
if we need those celestial guidance systems

striking mountaintops or if we need fuzzy
philosophy's abstruse failed reasonings: isn't

it simple and elegant enough to believe in
qualities, simplicity and elegance, pitch in a

little courage and generosity, a touch of
commitment, enough asceticism to prevent

fattening: moderation: elegant and simple
moderation: trees defined themselves (into

various definitions) through a dynamics of
struggle (hey, is the palaver rapping, yet?)

and so it is as if there were a genetic
recognition that a young tree would get up and

through only through taken space (parental
space not yielding at all, either) and, further:

so, trunks, accommodated to rising, to reaching
the high light and deep water, were slender

and fast moving, and this was okay because
one good thing about dense competition is that

if one succeeds with it one is buttressed by
crowding competitors; that is, there was little

room for branches, and just a tuft of green
possibility at the forest's roof: but, now,

I mean, take my yard maple—put out in the free
and open—has overgrown, its trunk

split down from a high fork: wind has
twisted off the biggest, bottom branch: there

was, in fact, hardly any crowding and competition,
and the fat tree, unable to stop pouring it on,

overfed and overgrew and, now, again, its skin's
broken into and disease may find it and bores

of one kind or another, and fungus: it just
goes to show you: moderation imposed is better

than no moderation at all: we tie into the
lives of those we love and our lives, then, go

as theirs go; their pain we can't shake off;
their choices, often harming to themselves,

pour through our agitated sleep, swirl up as
no-nos in our dreams; we rise several times

in a night to walk about; we rise in the morning
to a crusty world headed nowhere, doorless:

our chests burn with anxiety and a river of
anguish defines rapids and straits in the pit of

our stomachs: how can we intercede and not
interfere: how can our love move more surroundingly,

convincingly than our premonitory advice

garbage has to be the poem of our time because
garbage is spiritual, believable enough

to get our attention, getting in the way, piling
up, stinking, turning brooks brownish and

creamy white: what else deflects us from the
errors of our illusionary ways, not a temptation

to trashlessness, that is too far off, and,
anyway, unimaginable, unrealistic: I'm a

hole puncher or hole plugger: stick a finger
in the dame (*dam*, damn, dike), hold back the issue

of creativity's flood, the forthcoming, futuristic,
the origins feeding trash: down by I-95 in

Florida where flatland's ocean- and gulf-flat,
mounds of disposal rise (for if you dug

something up to make room for something to put
in, what about the something dug up, as with graves:)

the garbage trucks crawl as if in obeisance,
as if up ziggurats toward the high places gulls

and garbage keep alive, offerings to the gods
of garbage, of retribution, of realistic

expectation, the deities of unpleasant
necessities: refined, young earthworms,

drowned up in macadam pools by spring rains, moisten
out white in a day or so and, round spots,

look like sputum or creamy-rich, broken-up cold
clams: if this is not the best poem of the

century, can it be about the worst poem of the
century: it comes, at least, toward the end,

so a long tracing of bad stuff can swell
under its measure: but there on the heights

a small smoke wafts the sacrificial bounty
day and night to layer the sky brown, shut us

in as into a lidded kettle, the everlasting
flame these acres-deep of tendance keep: a

free offering of a crippled plastic chair:
a played-out sports outfit: a hill-myna

print stained with jelly: how to write this
poem, should it be short, a small popping of

duplexes, or long, hunting wide, coming home
late, losing the trail and recovering it:

should it act itself out, illustrations,
examples, colors, clothes or intensify

reductively into statement, bones any corpus
would do to surround, or should it be nothing

at all unless it finds itself: the poem,
which is about the pre-socratic idea of the

dispositional axis from stone to wind, wind
to stone (with my elaborations, if any)

is complete before it begins, so I needn't
myself hurry into brevity, though a weary reader

might briefly be done: the axis will be clear
enough daubed here and there with a little ink

or fined out into every shade and form of its
revelation: this is a scientific poem,

asserting that nature models values, that we
have invented little (copied), reflections of

possibilities already here, this where we came
to and how we came: a priestly director behind the

black-chuffing dozer leans the gleanings and
reads the birds, millions of loners circling

a common height, alighting to the meaty streaks
and puffy muffins (puffins?): there is a mound,

too, in the poet's mind dead language is hauled
off to and burned down on, the energy held and

shaped into new turns and clusters, the mind
strengthened by what it strengthens: for

where but in the very asshole of comedown is
redemption: as where but brought low, where

but in the grief of failure, loss, error do we
discern the savage afflictions that turn us around:

where but in the arrangements love crawls us
through, not a thing left in our self-display

unhumiliated, do we find the sweet seed of
new routes: but we are natural: nature, not

we, gave rise to us: we are not, though, though
natural, divorced from higher, finer configurations:

tissues and holograms of energy circulate in
us and seek and find representations of themselves

outside us, so that we can participate in
celebrations high and know reaches of feeling

and sight and thought that penetrate (really
penetrate) far, far beyond these our wet cells,

right on up past our stories, the planets, moons,
and other bodies locally to the other end of

the pole where matter's forms diffuse and
energy loses all means to express itself except

as spirit, there, oh, yes, in the abiding where
mind but nothing else abides, the eternal,

until it turns into another pear or sunfish,
that momentary glint in the fisheye having

been there so long, coming and going, it's
eternity's glint: it all wraps back round,

into and out of form, palpable and impalpable,
and in one phase, the one of grief and love,

we know the other, where everlastingness comes to
sway, okay and smooth: the heaven we mostly

want, though, is this jet-hoveled hell back,
heaven's daunting asshole: one must write and

rewrite till one writes it right: if I'm in
touch, she said, then I've got an edge: what

the hell kind of talk is that: I can't believe
I'm merely an old person: whose mother is dead,

whose father is gone and many of whose
friends and associates have wended away to the

ground, which is only heavy wind, or to ashes,
a lighter breeze: but it was all quite frankly

to be expected and not looked forward to: even
old trees, I remember some of them, where they

used to stand: pictures taken by some of them:
and old dogs, specially one imperial black one,

quad dogs with their hier*archies* (another *archie*)
one succeeding another, the barking and romping

sliding away like slides from a projector: what
were they then that are what they are now:

toxic waste, poison air, beach goo, eroded
roads draw nations together, whereas magnanimous

platitude and sweet semblance ease each nation
back into its comfort or despair: global crises

promote internationalist gettings-together,
problems the best procedure, whether they be in the

poet warps whose energy must be found and let
work or in the high windings of sulfur dioxide:

I say to my writing students—prize your flaws,
defects, behold your accidents, engage your

negative criticisms—these are the materials
on your ongoing—from these places you imagine,

find, or make the ways back to all of us, the figure,
keeping the aberrant periphery worked

clear so the central current may shift or slow
or rouse adjusting to the neessary dynamic:

in our error the defining energies of cure
errancy finds: suffering otherwises: but

no use to linger over beauty or simple effect:
this is just a poem with a job to do: and that

is to declare, however roundabout, sideways,
or meanderingly (or in those ways) the perfect

scientific and materialistic notion of the
spindle of energy: when energy is gross,

rocklike, it resembles the gross, and when
fine it mists away into mystical refinements,

sometimes passes right out of material
recognizability and becomes, what?, motion,

spirit, all forms translated into energy, as at
the bottom of Dante's hell all motion is

translated into form: so, in value systems,
physical systems, artistic systems, always this

same disposition from the heavy to the light,
and then the returns from the light downward

to the staid gross: stone to wind, wind to
stone: there is no need for "outside," hegemonic

derivations of value: nothing need be invented
or imposed: the aesthetic, scientific, moral

are organized like a muff along this spindle,
might as well relax: thus, the job done, the

mind having found its way through and marked
out the course, the intellect can be put by:

one can turn to tongue, crotch, boob, navel,
armpit, rock, slit, roseate rearend and

consider the perfumeries of slick exchange,
heaving breath, slouchy mouth, the mixed

means by which we stay attentive and keep to
the round of our ongoing: you wake up thrown

away and accommodation becomes the name of your
game: getting back, back into the structure

of protection, caring, warmth, numbers: one
and many, singles and groups, dissensions and

cooperations, takings and givings—the dynamic
of survival, still the same: but why thrown

out in the first place: because while the
prodigal stamps off and returns, the father goes

from iron directives that drove the son away
to rejoicing tears at his return: the safe

world of community, not safe, still needs
feelers sent out to test the environment, to

bring back news or no news; the central
mover, the huge river, needs, too, to bend,

and the son sent away is doubly welcomed home:
we deprive ourselves of, renounce, safety to seek

greater safety: but if we furnish a divine
sanction or theology to the disposition, we

must not think when the divine sanction shifts
that there is any alteration in the disposition:

the new's an angle of emphasis on the old:
new religions are surfaces, beliefs the shadows

of images trying to construe what needs no
belief: only born die, and if something is

born or new, then that is not it, that is not
the it: the it is the indifference of all the

differences, the nothingness of all the poised
somethings, the finest issue of energy in which

boulders and dead stars float: for what
if it were otherwise and the it turned out to

be *something*, damning and demanding, strict and
fierce, preventing and seizing: what range of

choice would be given up then and what value
could our partial, remnant choices acquire then:

with a high whine the garbage trucks slowly
circling the pyramid rising intone the morning

and atop the mound's plateau birds circling
hear and roil alive in winklings of wings

denser than windy forest shelves: and meanwhile
a truck already arrived spills its goods from

the back hatch and the birds as in a single computer-
formed net plunge in celebration, hallelujahs

of rejoicing: the driver gets out of his truck
and wanders over to the cliff on the spill and

looks off from the high point into the rosy-fine
rising of day, the air pure, the wings of the

birds white and clean as angel-food cake: holy, holy,
holy, the driver cries and flicks his cigarette

in a spiritual swoop that floats and floats before
it touches ground: here, the driver knows,

where the consummations gather, where the disposal
flows out of form, where the last translations

cast away their immutable bits and scraps,
flits of steel, shivers of bottle and tumbler,

here is the gateway to beginning, here the portal
of renewing change, the birdshit, even, melding

enrichingly in with debris, a loam for the roots
of placenta: oh, nature, the man on the edge

of the cardboard-laced cliff exclaims, that there
could be a straightaway from the toxic past into

the fusion-lit reaches of a coming time! our
sins are so many, here heaped, shapes given to

false matter, hamburger meat left out

scientists plunge into matter looking for the
matter but the matter lessens and, looked too

far into, expands away: it was insubstantial all
along; that is, boulders bestir; they

are "alive" with motion and space: there is a
riddling reality where real hands grasp each

other in the muff but toward both extremes the
reality wears out, wears thin, becomes a reality

"realityless": this is satisfactory, providing
permanent movement and staying, providing the

stratum essential with an essential air, the
poles thick and thin, the middles, at interchange:

the spreader rakes a furrow open and lights a
drying edge: a priestly plume rises, a signal, smoke

like flies intermediating between orange peel
and buzzing blur: is a poem about garbage garbage

or will this abstract, hollow junk seem beautiful
and necessary as just another offering to the

high assimilations: (that means up on top where
the smoke is; the incinerations of sin,

corruption, misconstruction pass through the
purification of flame:) old deck chairs,

crippled aluminum lawn chairs, lemon crates
with busted slats or hinges, strollers with

whacking or spinningly idle wheels: stub ends
of hotdogs: clumps go out; rain sulls deep

coals; wind slams flickers so flat they lose
the upstanding of updraft and stifle to white

lingo—but oh, oh, in a sense, and in an
intention, the burning's forever, O eternal

flame, principle of the universe, without which
mere heaviness and gray rust prevail: dance

peopling the centers and distances, the faraway
galactic slurs even, luminescences, plasmas,

those burns, the same principle: but here on
the heights, terns and flies avoid the closest

precincts of flame, the terrifying transformations,
the disappearances of anything of interest,

morsel, gobbet, trace of maple syrop, fat
worm: addling intensity at the center

where only special clothes and designated
offices allay the risk, the pure center: but

down, down on the lowest appropinquations, the
laborsome, loaded vessels whine like sails in

too much wind up the long ledges, the whines
a harmony, singing away the end of the world

or spelling it in, a monstrous surrounding of
gathering—the putrid, the castoff, the used,

the mucked up—all arriving for final assessment,
for the toting up in tonnage, the separations

of wet and dry, returnable and gone for good:
the sanctifications, the burn-throughs, ash free

merely a permanent twang of light, a dwelling
music, remaining: how to be blessed are mechanisms,

procedures that carry such changes! the
garbage spreader gets off his bulldozer and

approaches the fire: he stares into it as into
eternity, the burning edge of beginning and

ending, the catalyst of going and becoming,
and all thoughts of his paycheck and beerbelly,

even all thoughts of his house and family and
the long way he has come to be worthy of his

watch, fall away, and he stands in the presence
of the momentarily everlasting, the air about

him sacrosanct, purged of the crawling vines
and dense vegetation of desire, nothing between

perception and consequence here: the arctic
terns move away from the still machine and

light strikes their wings in round, a fluttering,
a whirling rose of wings, and it seems that

terns' slender wings and finely-tipped
tails look so airy and yet so capable that they

must have been designed after angels or angels
after them: the lizard family produced man in

the winged air! man as what he might be or might
have been, neuter, guileless, a feathery hymn:

the bulldozer man picks up a red bottle that
turns purple and green in the light and pours

out a few drops of stale wine, and yellowjackets
burr in the bottle, sung drunk, the singing

not even puzzled when he tosses the bottle way
down the slopes, the still air being flown in

in the bottle even as the bottle dives through
the air! the bulldozer man thinks about that

and concludes that everything is marvelous, what
he should conclude and what everything is: on

the deepdown slopes, he realizes, the light
inside the bottle will, over the weeks, change

the yellowjackets, unharmed, having left lost,
not an aromatic vapor of wine left, the air

percolating into and out of the neck as the sun's
heat rises and falls: all is one, one all:

hallelujah: he gets back up on his bulldozer
and shaking his locks backs the bulldozer up

dew shatters into rivulets on crunched cellophane
as the newly-started bulldozer jars a furrow

off the mesa, smoothing and packing down:
flattening, the way combers break flat into

speed up the strand: unpleasant food strings down
the slopes and rats' hard tails whirl whacking

trash: I don't know anything much about garbage
dumps: I mean, I've never climbed one: I

don't know about the smells: do masks mask
scent: or is there a deodorizing mask: the

Commissioner of Sanitation in a bug-black Caddy
hearse-long glisters creepy up the ziggurat: at

the top his chauffeur pops out and opens the
big back door for him: he goes over a few feet

away, puts a stiff, salute-hand to his forehead
and surveys the distances in all depths: the

birds' shadows lace his white sleeve: he
rises to his toes as a lifting zephyr from the

sea lofts a salt-shelf of scent: he approves: he
extends his arm in salute to the noisy dozer's

operator, waves back and forth canceling out
any intention to speak, re-beholds Florida's

longest vistas, gets back into the big buggy
and runs up all the windows, trapping, though,

a nuisance of flies: (or, would he have run
the windows down: or would anyone else have:

not out there: strike that:) rightness, at
any rate, like a benediction, settles on the

ambiance: all is proceeding: funding will be
continued: this work will not be abandoned:

this mound can rise higher: things are in order
when heights are acknowledged; the lows

ease into place; the wives get back from the laundromat,
the husbands hose down the hubcaps; and the

seeringly blank pressures of weekends crack
away hour by hour in established time: in your

end is my beginning: the operator waves back
to the Commissioner, acknowledging his understanding

and his submission to benign authority, and falls
to thinking of his wife, née Minnie Furher, a woman

of abrupt appetites and strict morals, a woman
who wants what she wants legally, largely as a

function of her husband's particulars: a closet
queen, Minnie hides her cardboard, gold-foiled

crown to wear in parade about the house when
nobody's home: she is so fat, fat people

like to be near her: and her husband loves
every bit of her, every bite (bit) round enough to get

to: and wherever his dinky won't reach, he finds
something else that will: I went up the road

a piece this morning at ten to Pleasant Grove
for the burial of Ted's ashes: those above

ground care; those below don't: the sun was
terribly hot, and the words of poems read out

loud settled down like minnows in a shallows
for the moment of silence and had their gaps

and fractures filled up and healed quiet: into
the posthole went the irises and hand-holds of dirt:

spring brings thaw and thaw brings the counterforce
of planted ashes which may not rise again,

not as anything recognizable as what they leach
away from: oh, yes, yes, the matter goes on,

turning into this and that, never the same thing
twice: but what about the spirit, does it die

in an instant, being nothing in an instant out of
matter, or does it hold on to some measure of

time, not just the eternity in which it is not,
but does death go on being death for a billion

years: this one fact put down is put down
forever, is it, or for forever, forever to be a

part of the changes about it, switches in the
earth's magnetic field, asteroid collisions,

tectonic underplays, to be molten and then not
molten, again and again: when does a fact end:

what does one do with this gap from just yesterday
or just this morning to fifty-five billion

years—to infinity: the spirit was forever
and is forever, the residual and informing

energy, but here what concerns us is this
manifestation, this man, this incredible flavoring and

building up of character and éclat, gone,
though forever, in a moment only, a local

event, infinitely unrepeatable: the song of
the words subsides, the shallows drift away,

the people turn to each other and away: motors
start and the driveways clear, and the single

fact is left alone to itself to have its first
night under the stars but to be there now

for every star that comes: we go away who must
ourselves come back, at last to stay: tears

when we are helpless are our only joy: but
while I was away this morning, Mike, the young

kid who does things for us, cut down the
thrift with his weedeater, those little white

flowers more like weedsize more than likely:
sometimes called cliff rose: also got the grass

out of the front ditch now too wet to mow, slashed:
the dispositional axis is not supreme (how tedious)

and not a fiction (how clever) but plain (greatness
flows through the lowly) and a fact (like as not)

a pain in the knee or hipjoint or warps and
knots in the leg muscles, even strange, binding

twinges in the feet ought to cause you to include
in the list of possibilities that that the high

arch in one of your feet has slipped, shortening
you shortlegged, your weight misdistributed,

your organs and moves skewed: of
course, if you already had a broken arch in

the other foot, then with both feet flat, you
should notice a considerable improvement of

sorts: if you were longlegged in one leg
and the foot of that leg went flat then you

might be overwhelmed with improvement of still
another kind: but, of course, if then the

short leg shortened to a flat foot, you'd be
back in dutch and puzzled by the consequences

especially if you knew nothing of the causes:
things are sustained by interrelations and

variety but when something goes wrong who
can isolate the active cause, an

active ingredient often riding in a complex of
contextual vectors: and nothing short of a

laboratory experiment in which controlled
circumstances can be evaluated one at a time

is likely to prove limitingly clarifying: I
was coming out of Goldwin Smith Hall after mail

call on a nova-bright late May day, the blues
and greens outdoing each other, when a dear friend

said, come and see, it's Ralph, he's in the car, and
thinking, I've never been asked to come see

Ralph before, I said, is anything the
matter, and she said, terminal cancer of the brain,

and I said, terminal cancer of the brain, and
she said, I found out a week ago, but don't say

anything to him: so, in the glaring light, his
window rolled down, I was talking with an old friend

as if the past twenty-five years of all three of us
as colleagues had shifted out of reach: everything

is theater and eternity is nothing at
all: yesterday, a man whose picture I'd just

seen in the local paper was going into the basement
of Lincoln Hall when I said, I saw that piece

about you in the paper, isn't that an early
retirement: I'm 63, he said: so'm I, I said:

my wife isn't well, he said, we want to travel;
do you think about retiring: all the time, I

said, but to what: departments grow haired and blackhaired
and shade away into white and dome-shine *at the top*:

the dissolve moves through tenure, or a job elsewhere,
part time, retirement, death: there never is

a department really but a slow flow you can't step
in twice: on writing a poem—you sit vacant and
relaxed (if possible), your mind wandering

freely, unengaged and in search of focus: you
may sit this way for several minutes till the

void unsettles you a bit and you become impatient
with the intrusion of an awareness of yourself

sitting with a touch of unwelcome exasperation
over a great blank: but you keep your mind

open and on the move and eventually there is a
trace of feeling like a bit of mist on a backroad

but then it reappears stronger and more central,
still coming and going, so the mind can't

grab it and hold on to it: but the mind begins
to make an effort, to shed from itself all

awareness except that of going with the feeling,
to relax and hold the feeling—the feeling

is a brutal burning, a rich, raw urgency:
the mind knows that it is nothing without the

feeling, so concentrating on the feeling, it
dreams of imminent shapes, emergences, of

clust'ral abundances, of free flow, forms discernible,
material, concrete, shapes on the move, and

then the mind gives way from its triggering, and
the mechanisms of necessity fall into, grasping the

upheaval, the action of making; the presence
of pressure appears, forces open a way, the

intensity heightens, groans of anguish and
satisfaction break from the depths of the

body, and the sweet dream occurs, the work
payloads, the fall-away slips through, the body

contracts and returns, ease lengthens throughout
the byways, and the mind picks up on the

environment again, turns to the practical
policing of the scene, restores itself to

normalcy and the objective world, the body hitching
itself up on the way: shit fire (and save matches):

we wheeled down the long glide from the mountains
into Wheeling: morning fog smoked away the tops

of hills and a river (or two) confluencing slashed
across by scary iron bridges jammed the narrowed

valley road, when the big black mouth of a tunnel
suddenly opened out of fog in solid rock, all the

events at once happening in the shakes: but then going
on down Route 7 along the Ohio; mammoth standings

of steam, way out of size, too solid to vanish, oozed
up from the nuclear craters, so much so tall that even

on our side of the river the outsized opal shades
of steam broke across us, shadowing us once and again:

slows like flying by or trying to drive to a mountain,
the far ahead lingering far behind: the freeway of

refineries, chemical steams, the gross companies
toughening the banks down by the banks of the O-hi-o.

is it all going to be like this: you wake up
in the morning and there is that: the next

morning, it's something else, and none of it
makes much sense: and then one day the weight

whomps down and you jack-spring onto a
different floe or the road you were doing seventy

on rumbles or runs out of road:
meanwhile, baked potatoes are still fine,

split down the middle, buttered up, the two white
cakes steaming, the butter (or sour cream) oozing

down and sex is, if any, good, and there's that time
between dawn and day when idle birds assert song

whereas a little while later they're quiet at
hunt or nest: and when during the drying out after

rains the trickle in the ditch bottom
quivers by a twig-built strait, the

wonder of it all returns, the separations, *ditches*?
ditches? rain?, a self?, a self?, being

here?, where?, here?, where's here?, splits, slices,
slits; quick-cut, overlapping dialog; a series of

declining peaks; dwindlings of a woman's bushy
head as if caught in a brush fire:

I have seen the future; it just went by, put
away: it advertises strokes, hip replacements,

insulin shots, sphygmomanometers or digital
punches: there is an end to delays and

remedies, regimens, and rehabs; another
pathology interrupts following on pathology:

terrible descriptions of outcomes appear here
and there, and outcomes, around which, though,

humor glints or boundless guffaws roll combers:
we're trash, plenty wondrous: should I want

to say in what the wonder consists: it is a tiny
wriggle of light in the mind that says, "go on":

that's what it says: that's all it says: river
edges clear up into furrows: the spear lengthens

till fish can't outleap its accuracay: what is
most beyond what is most beyond must be seen into:

love must be held still a minute to see if anything
can be said about it: if one negative will do,

will two negatives do more, more than two affirmatives:
shall the lines continue to move a little in sum longer:

but if a lake can look glassy, can't a building: it's
just a little piece of translucent, whitish light,

it wriggles, it is like, say, one meander, one whole
meander that came from nowhere and goes nowhere

but it wriggles and guess what it says: have I
cajoled you lately that I wantya: I'm none too

interested in regions because there's plenty of
spelled-out cultural differentiation in isolationisms,

and, anyhow, it's passing: I'm interested in the
differentiations of which there are now few that the

whole globe can belong to: precarious abstraction will
have to be the world's feed for a long time

before the little bits, so few, of concretion
and worldwide specification begin to appear,

but, tough scanty, growing and leading into a
growing world, not one spent: globe-round—

one thinks, slapping down the lines, making time
with eternity, one will thrive beyond the brink but

beyond the brink is no recollection but a wide
giving way into silver that filters farther away

into nothing: ghosts haunt the fields and hills,
the moon-soaked woodpaths, the misty cattail bogs

the littlest time, for they are attracted to the
light, the one a little farther on, a little farther,

and the light pulls them all away, and then, who knows,
becomes a rose wasted, perhaps, on the backside of

some barn, the summary rose rambled unseen: have
you stopped to think what existence is, to be here

now where so much has been or is yet to come and
where isness itself is just the name of a segment

of flow: stop, think: millennia jiggle in your eyes
at night, the twinklers, eye and star: the glistening

on the leaves when morning dew runs, little streaks
that head into drops, nodding leaves: think how

fine a motion sensation is, that it sweeps the nerves
and aligns the body's every cell because another

exists: all the bets are off if
pain is walking around the table cutting you or

someone else up, or if poverty has worked its way
up into your knees or you can't get your eyes dry,

or a child is bruised or a woman cornered
or thrills and violence can't be distinguished:

then existence recalls with relief that existence
ends, that our windy houses crack their frames

and spill, that nothing, not even cold killing bothers
the stars: twinkle, twinkle: just a wonder:

I say, globe-round selfempowerment like this could
be difficult and, perhaps, dangerous in the actual, but

these ways of words merely trace out designs
many can split up the filling in of: I punched

out Garbage at the library and four titles
swept the screen, only one, Garbage Feed,

seeming worth going on to; and that was about
feeding swine right: so I punched Garbage Disposal

and the screen came blank—nothing! all those
titles, row on row, of western goodies, mostly

worse than junk, but not a word on Disposal: I
should have looked, I suppose, under Waste Disposal

but, who cares, I already got the point: I
know garbage is being "disposed" of—but what

I wanted I had gotten, a clear space and pure
freedom to dump whatever, and this means most

of the catalog must go, so much that what is
left will need no computer to be kept track of:

har: words are a specialization on sound
making a kind of language: but there are many

not just languages but kinds of language: the
bluejay's extensive vocabulary signals states

of feeling or being—alarm, exasperation,
feeding, idleness—and the signal systems

lay out the states for the safety of sharing
by others, alerting to danger, even sharing

food sources: whales' pod-songs keep intimate
transactions fluid: horses neigh, whinny, and

snuffle (coach): elephants network even distant
air with sound waves too low for us to hear:

oh, no: we are not alone in language: we may
be alone in words, at least, almost alone in

speaking them, not alone (Koko) in understanding
them, at least reacting to them: we are nearly

alone in words: but the words do for us what other
languages do for others—they warn, inform,

reassure, compare, present: we may be alone in
words but we are not singular in language:

have some respect for other speakers of being and
for god's sake drop all this crap about words,

singularity, and dominion: it is so boring,
when I hear it a hook of anger in my guts tears

the lining: the world was the beginning
of the world; words are a way of fending in the

world: whole languages, like species, can
disappear without dropping a gram of earth's

weight, and symbolic systems to a fare you well
can be added without filling a ditch or thimble:

our cousins the birds talk in the morning: I
can tell the weather by their voices before

I open my eyes: I know some of their "words"
because I know, share with them, their states

of being and feeling: my cousins the
robins tug worms up from the lawn and eat them

and that gives me a piece of conflictual reality
until I savor the hog in my bacon, admire the

thighbone in my chicken: when the hens used to
sing in the spring laying into their ladders,

the windy courtship time of mating and
nesting, I can hear the singing now, the good

times: I know the entire language of chickens,
from rooster crows to biddy cheeps: it is a

language sufficient to the forms and procedures
nature assigned to chicken-birds but a language,

as competition goes, not sufficient to protect
them from us: our systems now

change their genes, their forms and procedures,
house them up in all-life houses, trick their

egg laying with artificial days and nights:
our language is something to write home about:

but it is not the world: grooming does for
baboons most of what words do for us.

sometimes old people snap back into life for a
streak and start making plans, ridiculous, you know,

when they will suddenly think of death again
and they will see their coffins plunge upward

like whales out of the refused depths of their
minds and the change will feel so shockingly

different—from the warm movement of a possibility
to a cold acknowledgment—they will seem not

to understand for a minute: at other times
with the expiration of plans and friends and

dreams and with the assaults on all sides of
relapses and pains, they will feel a

smallish ambition to creep into their boxes
at last and lid the light out and be gone,

nevermore, nevermore to see again, let alone
see trouble come on anyone again: oh, yes, there

are these moods and transitions, these bolt
recollections and these foolish temptations and

stratagems to distract them from the
course: this is why they and we must keep our

minds on the god-solid, not on the vain silks
and sweets of human dissipation, no, sirree:

unless of course god is immanent in which case
he may be to some slight extent part of the

sweets, god being in that case nothing more than or
as much as energy at large, a hair of it caught

in candy: I just want you to know I'm perfectly
serious much of the time: when I kid around

I'm trying to get in position to be serious:
my daffydillies are efforts to excuse the

presumption of assumption, direct address, my
self-presentation: I'm trying to mean what I

mean to mean something: best for that is a kind
of matter-of-fact explicitness about the facts:

best of all, facts of action: actions, actions,
actions, human or atomic: these actions cut

curves out in space, spiral up or in, turn and
turn back, stall, whirl: these are the motions

we learn from, these are the central figures,
this is the dance, here attitude and character,

precision and floundering lay out for us to see
their several examples, comically wasteful, as

with clowns or young squirrels playful at dusk:
here is the real morality, the economy of

action and reaction, of driving ahead, of going
slow, of walking the line, the tightrope, here

the narratives of motion that tell the story
the stories figure into facticity: let's

study the motions, are they slovenly, choppy,
attenuating, high, meandering, wasteful: we

need nothing more, except the spelling out of
these for those inattentive or too busily lost

in the daily elaborations to prize the essential:
(1) don't complain—ills are sufficiently

clear without reiterated description: (2) count
your blessings, spelling them over and over into

sharp contemplation: (3) do what you can—
take action: (4) move on, keep the mind

allied with the figurations of ongoing: when
I was a kid I always, it seemed, had a point

I couldn't say or that no one could accept—
I always sounded unconvincing; I lost the

arguments. people became impatient and stuck
to their own beliefs; my explanations struck

them as strange, unlikely: when I learned
about poetry, I must have recognized a means

to command silence in them, the means so to
combine thinking and feeling, imagination and

movement as to spell them out of speech:
people would buy the enchantment and get the

point reason couldn't, the point delivered below
the level of argument, straight into the fat

of feeling: so I'm asking you to help me, now:
yield to this possibility: I'm going to try to

say everything all over again: I've discovered
at sixty-three that the other thing I wished of

poetry, that it prevent death, has kept me a
little strange, that I have not got my feet out

of the embranglements of misapplication and out
into a clear space to go; that I have to start

again from a realization of failure: in fact,
having learned about commanding silence and

having, mostly by accident, commanded it a few
times, I've become afraid of convincingness,

what harm it can do if there is too much of
it along with whatever good, so I am now a

little uncertain on purpose: I recognize cases
in other words from time to time that I'd rather

see go through than my own: they seem wiser
cases: they come from people who seem better

wrapped around their spines: when their mouths
are open, their vertebrae form a sounding

foundation for their words: I have never,
frankly, grown up, not if growing up means I

wouldn't trade in what I have today for something
I might get tomorrow: I'm a trader: I'm still

looking for the buy to go all the way with:
I've become convinced that I don't have

anything particularly to convince anybody of: my
rhetoric goes on, though, with a terrible

machine-like insistence whether potholes
appear in the streets or not, or knots in my

line, or furriers in my traps: the trap shut
displeases no prey: pray you, go ahead around

me; I'm letting go a few springs and bolts from
my current mechanism: I'm getting down: I'm

not recommending more altitude than wings, not
anymore, not lately: no, no: not on your life.

you don't want to succeed too early and live
in the shadow of your own peek, peak, pock,

pork, puke: did I use the one about, the purpose
of being alive is to be alive: or the one about

the wildlife around here sometimes gets to be
pretty wild: this yellow tabby, not a kaffir,

not a burmese, not a blue point siamese, not a
striped manx, but just some old yellow cat

come over here in our yard and stakes out the
chipmunk or the garage mouse or rabbits or

squirrels: since we don't have a cat of our
own, his irregular visits keep the prey items

puzzled: so yesterday morning, I saw the
yellow settling in by the big yew and the

sniffy rabbit came up the other side of the
(look, how many lines are ending in *the*)

house on the driveway and when he turned into
the backyard, the tabby dived out for him and

in a few lean spreads of limbs just missed him:
the rabbit did not take off down the permanent

road: he moved off just far enough away to be
out of range of a cat sprint, and he sat still

as the world can get, subduing, I suppose, his
patting heart's fear in the very midst of fear: for—

well, there's one *chipmunk* you won't see
streaking around here anymore, plunging into

cement holes by the back steps or into ground
holes by the hydrangea or scrambling into the

crack under the middle post of the garage:
because (this is late the same day) I just saw

tabby walking away with him in his mouth: not
a white longhair, not an abyssinian, not a

calico, not a chat, but tabby, putting the
chipmunk down by the day-lilies, hardly yet having

their days, on the back hedge and then in
thrusting gulps and crunches downing chippy:

it is the law of the jungle we have learned so
much from: but some would say the purpose of

living is to serve others or rule them, or to
write music, and some would say that being alive

is like being dead, but I would say that the
purpose though it might not always—or but

seldom—come through is still being alive: I'm
a little shook up about the chipmunk: the other

day just before sunset, I watched him for
several minutes as he sat near the steps on the

backporch in the full sun and looked around a
bit now and then with an, taking in an, unprecedented

leisure and pleasure, the sunlight nearly coming
clear pink through his ears and forefeet: times

sometimes darken before dark: I'm running too many
threads and dropping too many stitches in this

weaving which is about, what, *life* and, mais oui,
death, wildlife and broken (tamed) verse: the

rabbit knows that if he doesn't like it here he
can't just go off somewhere else to live: so

he carefully dissolves from panic and nibbles
a sprig of weed, eases into a forward move,

and *lives in fear*: not helplessly, but in the
knowledge of his capabilities, his devices, his

bounces and split swerves: and he has young to
beget and young to raise and this without

benefit of tenure, estate, living trust, term
insurance, or social security: he is naked every

minute to clover tip or onslaught; onslaught
here meaning being chewed up: garbage disposal

has become more sweetly if broadly waste disposal
and guess what's two percent of permanent waste,

yep, disposable diapers, good to last
five hundred years: cute little babies' shit:

rambling thunderstorms in morning's blue darknesses—
such poetry, drumming and puddling:

snakes of currency head up and head out down
the driveway and off the sidewalk into the

spearmint: the sky whams and bangs, splits
with light: dense rain shuts out the trees

that reappear ghostly in a drizzle: birds, animals
lie quiet (birds twig up), enduring's acceptance, the

waiting out of the passage: reminding me of
Ole Liz who used to work in the fields—when

the big afternoon thunderheads found
her out cropping tobacco, she'd say, "When the

Lawd work, Ole Liza gone sit down"—and she would
not work while the majestic procedures of hail

and heaven went by: well-fed, the cat tucks in
feet, brings tail around, and dozes right out

in the open where the prey can be totally puzzled
by his indifference: prey move warily into this

ambiguity with a brave speculation, learning not
always to be terrified by a presence: and just

then, of course, or soon after, maybe even not
until the next morning, the dozing ends, and

if he doesn't look out so ends poor chipmunkey:
keep the open stare of the chill factor in warmth:

even in the midst of passion plant the seed
whose vine or tree may hang you: things

not followed as risks are risky: being alive
means being alive to mischance's chances.

in your end is my beginning, I repeat; also,
my end; my end is, in fact, your end, in a way:

are we not bound together by our ends: and when,
end to end, our ends meet, then we begin to

see the end of disturbing endlessness: unity
does what unity can: while preserving two

it accords in mutuality a mist wonderfully and
onefully coming together in—ah—well, why

entail sophistry: air and earth join, as you have
often read, via sculpted stone on a high platform

of the Old Peak: weight at great height fines
out into a kind of buoyance and one's feet feel

slippery and groundless: the material
spiritualizes and lock stone and air meet

cordially with a high lust clamping one to the other:
I must be at the crux of the matter: I do not

feel I can go on: progression lies down in the
ditches of inpouring doubt: I think of this tape

(this is another tape, a little wider, just about
pentameter) as the showboat churning down the

Mississippi with the banks, the fast currents,
the sandbars, drenchings; that is, it is going

down, like it or not, and I am like an analyst
or critic of action or behavior; I am saying,

is she into her depth; did she pack in enough
fuel to make it; shouldn't you nudge the bow

a touch starboard: and such like: such
as, why is she doing this; where did

she, and when, acquire this sense of mission:
I know boats don't have senses of mission:

but you were going along with it, weren't you:
I'm afraid a yaw will get out of hand

and the stern will swing around on the bow, and
we'll be wheeling in reverse, as if in

reverse, in order to progress forward backward:
it doesn't really matter: hurricanes have hit

inland far enough to drive boats of any size
right up on river shores: and boats have had to

wait weeks, at times, for rain or for a wall
arriving downstream from a flood elsewhere:

I read *Life on the Mississippi* a long time ago
and those boats were harder to steer than this:

still, it's rough for anyone in a fog, and
mark twains all over the place are hardly

reassuring: but it's okay: we're going far
away soon into space, and ships will roll

and enmeshments of asteroids or stellar dust
confuse speed: it doesn't matter: we'll get

seed off this primordial hulk before we drown
it in throwaways: we have a spirit that

clears after every stupidity, designs treads for
offroaders, matches the right bacterium to the

right poison: I just wish neanderthal were still
here: I would have loved those rugged little

four-foot fellows: imagine having a nest
of workers down in the basement, sturdy little

whippersnappers to run errands: first thing you
know the muvahs are fucking your mother, in laws,

so, so much for neanderthals' brisk hard nuts: I
think I'm at the crux right now: I can hardly think

or think of hardly a thing to say: I've searched
my mind for swerves of narrative, minor

assemblages of incident on a string, emblems of
the shapes of actions, the essential displaying

the newspapery: sometimes, just when you think
the spirit is going to rise, something else does:

life, life is like a poem: the moment it
begins, it begins to end: the tension this

establishes makes every move and moment, every
gap and stumble, every glide and rise significant:

for if life or poem went dribbling endlessly
on, what identifiable arc or measure could it

clarify: within limits the made thing accepts
its revelation and dissolution, its coming and

going, beginning and ending, being and nonbeing:
the poem moves through the smooth or astonished

beginning, the taking on of engagement and
complication, the gathering up of direction and

possibility, and the falling out and fading
away: this is all so reasonable, we sometimes

wonder why grief tells us so we wanted to cling
to being, the good things, oh, the good things,

but in real life as in real poems clarifying
form, such as the beginning and ending of the

trip to Mexico (with the middle at San Miguel
de Allende, double-middled by a week in Mexico

City) are minor forms within larger constructs
not so clear: big segments crack off—say,

when you moved from Allentown to Albuquerque
or when the divorce first was named—giving

you impressions, among others, of irrelevancies,
hacked up intuitions, but also false, to some

extent, notions of recency—your *late* departure,
the house you *just* sold—and when that is

blanked out of memory, life is shortened and
you are young in a new time, pure local lyrics

coexistent with what appears to be a whole
shambles, the shambles questioning the lyric

out of easy shape, and the lyric providing
intervals of symmetry in the jumbled enlargement,

but it is subservient when art imitates life;
art makes life, just as it makes itself, an

imitation: art makes shape, order, meaning,
purpose where there was none, or none discernible,

none derivable: life, too, if it is to have
meaning, must be made meaningful: if it is to

have purpose, its purpose must be divined, invented,
manifested, held to: a wallow is a wallow:

who knows: everything here may be meaninglessly
prevalent so as to give us the potential of

making's range: when we bawl over our
predicament we merely accuse ourselves: why

must we answer up to reality, when we can
axle reality into our illusions: not

delusional illusions but just the "turn"
toward the possible, the hope, the trust, the

belief: oh, well: argument is like dining:
mess with a nice dinner long enough, it's garbage.

an early June morning in early June, we, having
already gone out to breakfast, pop into the red

Toyota Tercel and breeze down the hill by Lake
Cayuga to the farmers' market, so bright, so

clear, rows and rows of cars and stalls and,
beyond, boats docked calm on the glassy inlet:

the people look a little ruffled, like yards
trying to come out of icebound winters into

springs, the old stalks still there, the space
of the new stuff not filled out: affliction

here, where the heavy woman, heavier than last
fall, leans over to swish one knock-knee past

(check that rhyme) the other; affliction there,
where the wobble-legged man leans over into his

arm crutches, a four-legged progression: aging
women, drooped breasts under loose T-shirts,

hair making a virtue of snow-white or veering
off into an original expression of blue:

toothless, big-bellied, bald, broad-rumped,
deaf: the afflicted, hurts hurting but less

than they hurt at home or, if hurting more,
with some compensation: one absolutely lovely

person, perhaps: the radiance of some babies'
faces, the perfect interest of some boy in mud

puddles: and this is all under the aspect of
eternity, soon to be: but listen to the

good-mornings and how've-you-beens and
were-you-away-any-of-the-winters, along with

the hanging baskets of fuchsia, purple and red
and streaked white, tuberous begonias with the

freshest colors alive, bread, and stall after
stall of vegetables, goat cheese, honey, coffee

plus a live minnequin who is moved to thank you
by coins and bills dropped in a hat: this is

we at our best, not killing, scheming, abusing,
running over, tearing down, burning up: why

did invention ever bother with all this, why
does the huge beech by the water come back every

year: oh, the sweet pleasures, or even the hope
of sweet pleasures, the kiss, the letter from

someone, the word of sympathy or praise, or just
the shared settled look between us, that here

we are together, such as it is, cautious and
courageous, wily with genuine desire, policed

by how we behave, all out of eternity, into
eternity, but here now, where we make the most

of it: I settle down: I who could have used
the world share a crumb: I who wanted the sky

fall to the glint in a passing eye: the crack
in the dome of knowledge, the aperture, so to

say, poetically speaking, into faith is, of
course, as everyone knows, the magical exception

to the naturalistic rule: derivations (pharma-
cological?) from nature do what they can, usually

with terrible side effects or with disjunctivitis
with other drugs (with, with) but one exception

as in rising in a fiery go-cart is lustfully
believed to overturn, or else to buoy, all

naturalism, by which is intended to be meant
sense, common and unusual varieties, science,

knowledge, craft: there is a web-worm falls
sometimes aslant the honeysuckle hedge in spring

breeze or other dislocation and finds itself
asquirm dangerously dangled in the open air (I've

seen hornets trim those babies right out of the
air): this one I paused to view was wrestling

up the single thread of web, nipping and tucking,
reaching up for a hold on the tight and bringing

itself up till the bit length could be added
to the tiny cotton ball gathered at its

head: but this is mere mechanics: down its
back was a purplish streak exactly the color

of honeysucklebushlimbstems, the top part (buds)
of the stems: his feet, his laterals, were

exactly the color of the lateralhoneysucklebush
limbstems: while this waits explanation, I

hold it a sufficient miracle, on which, tho,
I posit no faith of a kind but faith of another

kind: that is, maybe some spooky agency does
manage all: we're attracted to stars not because

they're confessional but because of the roles
they create into play; we're attracted to

pretend, not fact, first: then, the clothing
of creativity about the person attracts us to

his sins: we are awed and want the clay feet
to stop walking over us: also we want better

to understand how to reach this creativity's
sinfulness ourselves: so why can't poets

speak in tongues, others than their own; is
truth in the fact or in the persuasion, in the

credible action or the flat statement: I don't
care whether anybody believes me or not: I

don't know anything I want anybody to believe or
in: but if you will sit with me in the light

of speech, I will sit with you: I would rather
do this than eat your ice cream, go to a movie,

hump a horse, measure a suit, suit a measure:
I would at my age rather do this than

skateboard, but I can think of nothing I'd
rather do than think of skateboard loops out

of skateboard bowls, the various designs in the
momenta: the rising up in rounds over the rims.

a waste of words, a flattened-down, smoothed-
over mesa of styrofoam verbiage; since words were

introduced here things have gone poorly for the
planet: it's been between words and rivers,

surface-mining words and hilltops, cuneiform
records in priestly piles; between clay

tablets and irrigated fields: papyrus in
sheets; vellum in Alexandria; hundreds of

temples to type and, now, networks of words
intricate as the realities they represent:

a persiflageous empurpling: the rains clear,
the blue sky's ragged white clouds shine up

the greens of treetops: the driveway is thick
with sugarmaple seed the chipmunk fills his

pouches with fast: the spirea bush, the five
nearly round, slightly dented petals to each

blossom, snows the ground white during rains:
the norway maple I cut back in the hedge has

turned out leaves ten inches between the
points! the robin down by the fence just about

sings his head off now, close to dusk, his
belly lineated tight with slack worms: (yes, there's

a chipmunk left, though the tabby's lying out
for him): we must have the biggest machine,

fifty miles around, find the smallest particles,
and the ditchwork of the deepest degradation

reflects waters brighter than common ground:
poetry to no purpose! all this garbage! all

these words: we may replace our mountains with
trash: leachments may be our creeks flowing

from the distilling bottoms of corruption:
our skies, already browned, may be our brown

skies: fields may rise from cultivation into
suffocation: here was a silvery-green-blue-bright

planet, held in sway for hundreds of millions
of years by leathery monsters racing about roaring

and tearing, terrible cries of contest by
lakeshores in placid evenings, terrible cries of

assault at night, etc., all shoved away, imagine:
and then along came the frail one, our ancestor,

scavenger, seed finder, nut cracker, fruit
picker, grubs, bulbs, etc., and here we are at

last, last, probably, behold, we have replaced
the meadows with oilslick: when words have

driven the sludge in billows higher than our
heads—oh, well, by then words will have left

the poor place behind: we'll be settling
elsewhere or floating interminably, the universe

a deep place to spoil, a dump compaction will
always make room in! I have nothing to say:

what I want to say is saying: I want to be
singing, sort of: I want to be engaged with

the ongoing: but I have no portmanteau filled
with portfolio: still, I am for something:

what am I for: I'm for rights consistent with
others' rights: that says little but saying,

with a touch of singing: we'll live no more on
this planet, we'll live in the word: what:

we'll get off: we'll take it with us: our
equations will make any world we wish anywhere

we go: we'll take nothing away from here but
the equations, cool, lofty, eternal, that were

nowhere here to be found when we came: we are
a quite special species, as it were: would to

mercy those who went before in ignorance and
irresolution could know they forwarded a part,

though, of couse, had they been told they'd
not have believed it: imagine, though we think

ourselves purposeless, we may be the thinnest
cross-section of an upcoming announcement, and

though we cannot imagine what the purpose might
be, even now it may be extruding itself, tiny

threads of weak energy fields, right through
us: first an earth in peace; then, hundreds of

years looking for other wars: strife and peace,
love and grief, departure and return: gliding

we'll kick the *l* out of the wor*l*d and cuddle
up with the avenues and byways of the word:

the real trouble with a blabbermouth is that when
he talks and keeps talking, pretty soon he's

talking *around*, and pretty soon he's
on the other side! of where he was: a real man

doesn't say two words because that way he opens
the narrowest, which is the most convictive

avenue to identity you can imagine: he doesn't
fluff and fool, dip and weave, elaborate and

wander off into sophistic woods of ramification,
but a fool blabberer cannot believe all the

things he says himself, indeed he believes nothing
except the wisdom of agreeing with whomever he

meets: he can present a scaffolding exfoliation, a
splaying network of words that will accommodate the color

of any man's opinion, or woman's: in fact, the
blabberer is so without trace of any bias of

his own, he unwittingly does the good of feeling
out so many positions persons of opposing

words or twos can find themselves assembled in
a common place, and though they throw the

blabberer out, they make peace ungratefully in
the verbal provinces of a pure dissemblance:

of his making: and with the best blabberers,
this does not necessarily amount to circumlocution

some of the best succinct as hell and twice
as flashy: and a blabbermouth, wandering around

in disquisitional irresponsibility, can sashay
by your one or two words and contextualize them

(odd that the tillers of the soil here, the
earthworms, are the harvest (robins get them)
while the crop (grass) is thrown away): the

loudmouth, though, can be distinguished from
the blabbermouth in that loudness requires more

energy of formation and broader executions of
lip and jaw, slowing delivery and, in extreme

cases, tiring the speaker silent: though his
tenure is shortened, the loudmouth's audience

is compensatingly wider: where the blabbermouth
may be down to a kind of hissing even the

nearest have to strain to hear, the loudmouth
satisfactorily delivers effortlessly received

phraseology spanning hundreds: nothing is
perfect, unless you can unite two good sides from

different situations: to be a loudmouth
blabbermouth is to be a trifle above, a wonder:

there are those, also mixtures of good and bad
elements, who will say nothing: they will look

and fuck—nothing: they will eat a whole meal
and take half an hour to belch: these stolid

people are solid: they resemble blabbermouths
in a way in that they set up circumstances into

which you can read any message or from which
derive any picturation: but if the measure of

a man is not how much he says or how loud, I'm
sure I cannot imagine what to say next: a

thunderhead topping out at 65,000 feet can
deliver hailstones a foot deep into your field:

or golfball-size smokestones, the pollution,
you know: in the milky days of early June,

cone pollen so thick it hazes cars in an hour
and leaves broad yellow outlines to macadam

pools after rain—in those days, in those days
oh, yes, in those days: it is after all only

about what it is about: if it is mundane then
that is what it is: if it is mundane with an

element of the remarkable, an element of the
remarkable is with it: if it is mostly remarkable,

it is likely to be unlikely: the remarkable,
become occasional, wears unremarkable, and what

happens frequently hardly happens at all: I
looked into the pit of death and it was there,

the pit was, and the death: I circled it saying
this looks like safety's surcease next to which

risks' splits and roars, the sparrow's lone note
in the gray tree, are radiances: the rocks

came up to me in a wall saying they would say
nothing, and the trees bent away as in wind

their tops hanging on to silence, and I could
make nothing out in the brook's fuzzy bustle:

the bushes huddled down by the pinewoods as if
looking for a path leading in, with no saying

and no listening either, so I derived the nature
of each thing from itself and made each derivation

speak, the mountains quietly resounding and very
authoritative, their exalted air perfect grain

of the spiritual, the sense of looking down so
scary half-love for height held: I made tongues

for adder's-tongue, periwinkle, and jimminycricket;
they wagged, and these tongues rang in my head

as in a chanson delicate of essence and point:
an assemblage, a concourse of intercourse, a

recourse: what is it, that you would turn down
a prairie for it, the prairie said as I went

on, my eyes set longsighted, and the turtle
eased needlepoint airholes up from swampwater,

his eyes quizzical in a downturn, and said,
where else does the shadow of the logknots fall

more sharply dark on the water, but I didn't
have time to take time: I spent every coin I

had into the good business of my own burning:
one day the whirlwinds gathered in the flats by

the foot of a range and turned and turned for
some hours, sidling up alongside ravines or

skiddling out among the sharp bush to gather
more sand, or just standing around idly spinning

like elegant women put off somewhere without
hats, but dusk's blue called them off finally,

each to a separate valley, and by the time the
moon chipped the range line, all the conversation

of the day had become arroyo or talus stone,
motionless as a sun drinking distant water:

the next day the red-shouldered rusty hills
woke the whirlwinds, first wobbly and vague,

but, the sun creaking the rocks, taller and
slenderer than lombardies, and they elegantly

regathered in a far hollow of the plains and
spun all day, all day spinning and humming,

reaching so high their tops seemed to be
hollowing out holes in the sky: they hummed

continents' stories, hornets' nests of round
persuasions: they inched about in their spinning:

they pillared the sky but, when clouds of
conestogas or icebergs floated over, dissolved,

stringing undone: a weaving, a shuttle, a
fabric, a going staying where you are: the

whirlwind, not human, I'm the whirlwind: the
creaking hills, not human, my silence cracks and

creaks: the flow of clouds not mine, my
motions trained clear by clouds: and the

streams' yielding bending fathers my winding:
and the semicircles' gusts before storms make

grassclumps draw in the sand—these are the
going closures that organize mind, allowing

and limiting, my mind's ways: the rabbit's
leaps and halts, listenings, are prosody of

a poem floating through the mind's brush: I
mix my motions in with the mix of motions, all

motions cousins, conveyors, purveyors, surveyors,
rising from the land, eddying coils of a wash,

bristling with fine-backed black clarity as with
brookripples over stone, spreading out, evaporating

or seeping in under, soaking, salt flats, the
turkey buzzard whirling, the wind whirling,

the giant "stills" of the sea and I, and sand,
whirling, stalling, breaking out, getting on,

coming round—cousins, not silent, either,
communicative, but not with human sound,

communicative motions making sounds, much mutual
glistening in a breezy grove of spring aspen speech

take, in leavetaking, the leavings: feed your
bony dog, your cat stalking stiff in hunger-meows:

gather up the scraps for pig-swill: anything
thrown out to the chickens will be ground fine

in gizzards or taken underground by beetles and
ants: this will be transmuted into the filigree

of ant feelers' energy vaporizations: chunk and
smear, grease and glob will boil refined in

time's and guts' alembics, the air carbonized
rich, potash in lacy leavings' milding terrain:

a breadcrumb borne away by hundreds like a stone
waist-high many legs to the pyramid: but nothing

much can become of the clear-through plastic
lid: it finds hidden security in the legit

museums of our desecrations—the mounds, the
heights of discard: meaningless is the

providence, the wiping clear of planes where we
can structure possibility into whatever housings

level out: the antecedent of meaning is not
meaning always, meaning which could direct,

delimit, interfere, but the absence of meaning:
we should be pretty happy with the possibilities

and limits we can play through emergences free
of complexes of Big Meaning, but is there

really any meaninglessness, isn't meaninglessness
a funny category, meaninglessness missing

meaning, vacancy still empty, not any sort of
disordering, or miscasting or fraudulence of

irrealities' shows, just a place not meaning
yet—perhaps, of course, and appropriately,

never to mean: space, the terror of the
unimaginably empty and endless, distances stars,

for example, not to mention the core-fire of the
galaxy, so we cellular brushfires can burn cool

in a way-off arm: there is truly *only* meaning,
only meaning, meanings, so many meanings,

meaninglessness becomes what to make of so many
meanings: and, truly, everything is *real*, so

real, the climbing cloud-towers this morning,
each in its individual space so white-heighted,

silent, slow; the squirrel hide still lined here
and there with dried curls of meat, legbones

nearly outlined still in place, this out on the
lawn, tossed there perhaps from the road or

dragged in by a crow (a yardful of treesful of
raucous crows raising young every spring):

(here on the 10th it is so late into spring
it is nearly early summer: the big days turn,

hardly wobbling in time for a couple of weeks or
so around this widest day): the anthill has

erupted gray-dry in the grass and the little
black buggers are circulating outside and inside

tunnels, as in a cave weather or meshwork weather's
digestive, arterial systems; the universe, you

may know, may be backed up like water behind a
dam, and it may spill, as it already has from

ten to four dimensions, still lower anyday: still
the world is not a show consciousness can pull

off or wipe out: because consciousness can neither
wipe out nor actualize it it is not a show but

the world: if one does not eat perception-blasted
potato, one will blast perception by the loss of

perception: starch (in Arch) in the potato
meets with my chemistry to enliven my chemistry,

clear my eyes, harden, perhaps, my muscle, wag
my tongue (almost certainly): hallelujah: if

death is so persuasive, can't life be: it is
fashionable now to mean nothing, not to exist,

because meaning doesn't hold, and we do not exist
forever; this *is* forever, we are now in it: our

eyes see through the round time of nearly all
of being, our minds reach out and in ten billion

years: we are in so much forever, we pay it no
mind, we'd rather think of today's shopping or

next week's day off: but we will not be in
forever forever, that is the dropout: is it

too much to be in forever a while: dead we are
out of time and forever, both: I want to get

around to where I can say I'm glad I was here,
even if I must go: I want to believe that the

possibility given me to be here was not a betrayal
or trap or hoax but a trial of the possibility

of a possibility, that I can find firm grounds
for thinking what I want to think as well as

for despair, incoherence, distrust, drifting
acedia: nonreferentiality is a referentiality

of nonreferentiality: slap the world any way,
it flaps back: turn the dial past zero, it's

back to one: nonrepresentation is a representation
of nonrepresentation: things are awash in

ideality: ideal meaninglessness, ideal absurdity,
ideal ideals: we want to know the reality of

these perfectly, ideally, as themselves: poems
that give up the ideal of making sense do not

give up the ideal of not making sense: nom de
plumage best feathers a nest egg, ivory doorknob:

what are we to think of the waste, though: the
sugarmaple seeds on the blacktop are so dense,

the seedheads crushed by tires, the wings stuck
wet, they hold the rains, so there's no walkway

dry: so many seeds, and not one will make a
tree, excuse the expression: what of so much

possibility, all impossibility: how about the
one who finds alcohol at eleven, drugs at seventeen

death at thirty-two: how about the little
boy on the street who with puffy-smooth face and

slit eyes reaches up to you for a handshake:
supposing politics swings back like a breeze and

sails tanks through a young crowd: what about the
hopes withered up in screams like crops in

sandy winds: how about the letting out of streams
of blood where rain might have sprinkled into

roadpools: are we to identify with the fortunate
who see the energy of possibility as its necessary

brush with impossibility: who define meaning
only in the blasted landfalls of no meaning:

who can in safety call evil essential to the
differentiations of good: or should we wail

that the lost are lost, that nothing can be right
until they no longer lose themselves, until we've found

charms to call them back: are we to take no
comfort when so much discomfort turns here and

there helplessly for help: is there, in other
words, after the balances are toted up, is there

a streak of light defining the cutting edge as
celebration: (clematis which looks as dead and

drained in winter as baling wire transports in
spring such leaves and plush blooms!) I walked

down the hall to the ward-wing surrounded on
three sides with windows' light and there with

the other diabetics like minnows in the pool-
head of a tidal rising sat my father slumped,

gussied up with straps, in a wheelchair, a catheter leading
to the little fuel tank hung underneath, urine

the color of gasoline, my father like the
others drawn down half-asleep mulling over his

wheels: where, I thought, hope of good is gone
evil becomes the deliverer, and more evil, to get

one through to the clearing where presence, now
pain, enters oblivion: my father roused himself

and took some hope in me but then left me back
alone: at a point in evil, evil changes its

clothes and death with a soft smile crooks its
finger to us: a taking by death leaving the

living bereft: such a mixture! where does a steady
formulation settle down: what integration

of wisdom holds scoured by the bottoms of . . .
bottoms? . . . questioned, I mean, by nibbling

exception and branching direction: every balance
overbalances: judiciousness loses the excitement

of error: realizing that there is no safety
is safety: the other side of anything is worth

nearly as much as the side: the difference
so slight in fact, that one goes out to see if

it is there: I want a curvature like the
arising of a spherical section, a sweep that

doesn't break down from arc into word, image,
definition, story, thesis, but all these

assimilated to an arch of silence, an interrelation
permitting motion in stillness: I want to see

furrows of definition, both the centerings of
furrow and the clumpy outcastings beyond: I do

not want to be caught inside for clarity: I
want clarity to be a smooth long bend

disallowing no complexity in coming clean: why
do I want this, complexity without confusion,

clarity without confinement, time in time, not
time splintered: if you are not gone at a certain

age, your world is: or it is shriveled to a
few people who know what you know: aunts and

uncles with their histories blanked out, the thick
tissue of relationships erased into one of emptiness

or maybe your cousins, too, are gone, and
the world has starved to a single peak,

you and what you know alone, with no one
else in the world to nod recognizing what you

say and recall without explanation: so, have
your choice to leave the world or have it leave

you; either way you choose will bring the same
result, nothingness and the vanishment of

what was: over and over the world rolls in this
wise, so much so that people stricken with these

knowledges think the aspiration to win to be
remembered, to be let hanging, dibbling in the

minds of those continuing: but life is not first
for being remembered but for being lived! how

quaint and sad the lives of those who have lived
but are gone, the vacant sadness of two eternities

pressed together, squeezing them dry to
nondegradable remnants—trash: the meaning,

the tears, loves, sweet handholdings, all
the fears, jealousies, hangings, burnings—

throwaways, obsolescences that plug up
the circulations today, burdening the living

with guilty obligations of memory and service:
to have the curvature, though, one needs the

concisions of the local, contemplations such as
how to slice a banana for breakfast oatmeal,

fourteen thick or thirty-three thin events, the
chunky substance of fourteen encounters or the

flavor availabilities in limp circles: fly the
definite lest it lock you in! have solvent by

should the imperative devise you a vice: see
a spread of possibilities, not an onion plot:

the juggler has twice as many balls as hands
because it's all up in the air: keep it up

in the air, boundingly like ephemera at dusk:
or dawn: I saw in Carolina morning flies

midair like floating stones: the dew, heavy;
the sun, blood red: a road dipping round a

pine grove down a hill to a pond, the spillway
clogged with cattails bent with breezes and with

redwings awilding day: a crippled old farmer
up early with his dog, noon likely to melt tar,

a benchlong of old blacks at the crossroads
gas station, dogfennel high on the woods' edge,

some scraggly roastnear corn used up, tomato
plants sprawled out, become vines: morning,

gentlemen, how you all doing: these bitty
events, near pangs commonplace on this planet

so strangely turned out, we mustn't take on so
but let the music sway, the rhetoric ride, the

garbage heave, for if we allow one solid cast
of grief to flip and filter away into all the

trinklets it might go, we would be averaged
down to a multiple diminishment like acceptance:

but we mean to go on and go on till we unwind
the winding of our longset road, when, we

presume, the nothingness we
step to will mirror treasures we leave, a

strange mirror, everything in our lives having
taken root in love, the sequences having become

right because that is the way they had to run:
but, then, for the trouble of love, we may be

so tired that indifference will join ours to the
hills' indifference and the broad currents of

the deep and the high windings of the sky, and
we may indeed see the ease beyond our

understanding because, till now, always beyond

A bird dabbed me, a virgin soil, as I issued
out under the open blue this morning, and

thinking it beetle or moth, I brushed it off my
shoulder and smeared do on one or more digits:

my thoughts flew to geese dumps and the numbers
of rafts of geese I've seen over unsoiled:

do migrating geese not do do as they, sprinkling, go,
or are they so high their droppings achieve

vaporizing accelerations, like rocket launchers and
reentry cones, often part solid: or are there

not diarrhetic exceptions to control one might
have seen splat or been shloshed by: so many

specialities in our little knowledge: undone by
do, I forged on, noting the eternity of the

hill-line across the valley, uniting the ravines:
from Mérida, I'd keep vaguely north along

the valley, road and valley river tangling crossings,
down to where the road tends to the west and

rises back up toward the ridge before Valera.
I would rest a bit there or take a plane—

probably I would not take a plane but rent a
burro and go the long, small road on down to

Cabimas or Lago de Maracaibo, an excellent
shore, unfailingly warm: is there intermediacy

between hallucinatory flux and pure form's rigid
thought and count: between diarrhea and constipation,

how about chunky intermediacy, some motion with
minor forms clear, clusters or bindings, with the

concomitant gaps, tie-offs and recommencements
expected: could not a narrative be the speed

and dimensions, feel, of a progression: and
could there not be a blow away of emptiness:

and the stasis, unmoving, unfeeling: impaction:
a robin rows out of a tree across the road and

bombs a couple of dabs on the blacktop, as if
by dabs paying off flight: beads, actually:

but hitting the ground, the beads compress into disks
(little white disks) which peered into are alive

with bellyroundworms, intricate, worky, lily-white
flailing bellyworms, circumscribed in a sudden

dessication without wings: squirrels stop at
knotches to scratch and nuzzle: pests are all

over, and inside: if you've derived from life
a going thing called life, life has a right to

derive life from you: ticks, parasites, lice,
fleas, mites, flukes, crabs, mosquitoes, black

flies, bacteria: in reality, reality is like
still water, invisible, spiritual: the real

abides, spiritual, while entities come and go:
binds, warps, drives, with their accompanying

marvels, beauties, goals, solutions misconstrue
what we in time work out invisible again:

roundabout gives us a place to go: turbulence
livens our passion for clearing, clearing for

turbulence: is the ring of truth, however clear
and plain, superior to richness, to the beauty

of gooey language densely managed: or is truth
beauty, whenas so much truth is garbage by,

if by nothing else, obsolescence, obsolescence,
though, only a matter of habiliments, which are

on and off, not essentials: poverty, burningly
true, is not beautiful: order excusing cruelty

is not beautiful but plenty truthful: mounds
on held mounds as well as sinkholes and deep

transgressions of trash are not beautiful:
deformity, deviance, disease are often ugly,

yet it must be said (it makes no nevermind to
me if it makes no nevermind to you) that much

good writing, for example—containing within
itself, if not in its matter, its manner, much

truth and beauty and beauty and truth—has
derived under the resources of stressed attention

or perilous need compensations not justifying
suffering but smartening up a corner in it here

and there: things that go around sometimes go
around so far around they come back around: if you

like my form, experience my function: doctors
lost all their patients, help often barely

distinguishable from the forwarding: tone with
an undertow: obscure verse—am I supposed to

understand that I'm not supposed to understand
it or not: some of these short guys are so

wellhung they'd give an inch off their dicks
if they could put it under their heels, and you

could jack down some of these tall guys a foot
if they could move into another inch: and the

skinny-hipped women, double moons up front
while with some of these big rears, they don't

have enough to stick your lips to: these wayward
compensations reaching squandering extremes:

beauty is so much in demand it's a wonder natural
selection hasn't thinned out anything not perfectly

beautiful: but nature, if I may speak for it,
likes a broad spectrum approaching disorder so

as to maintain the potential of change with
variety and environment: the true shape of

perfect beauty, hard to find, somehow floats
implicit and stable there among the shorties,

flopsies, big-legged, limpy, skew-faced, etc.
and if any change comes along it's going to

find a possibility to jump on, you wait and see,
or I'm the biggest fool in the country: for

perfect beauty, narrowed down and reproduced,
might be a frail shield to an avalanche of

reorganization: I wonder if in the mind's
control of pain, the point of the farthest

projection draws in the sweetest ether,
disestablishes the local, perhaps internal,

crossing constructs, alleviates the focus of
the inwardly immediate, releasing sights of mind

into range's most easeful extreme: what design
ypointing could bring the stars answering news,

a ray so far and fine it, perhaps converging,
never closes on infinity, needle of the subtlest

conveyance: except if one needed to turn aside
to daily cares or, conceivably, joys, how

could one disjoint, decommission a headful of
spires, or get back from the most distant

contemplation of a single spire: the local
forms and bursts, releasing the immediate,

though: I watched last fall a squirrel over by
the ivy bank by the university, a scrap of his

tail lost to scrap, dig up a nut, roll it
round like a tool to his chippy teeth, the other

end from the scrappy tail grown fat and frizzly
white for winter, that warm, sunny morning in

early December: a fat coward, a territorial
bout, flight, and everything kept except a bit

(or bite) of tail, and a feast that morning in
a tranquillity of university ivy: (time allows

edgings into so many forms of reality, we let
them all go, they go anyway, but we keep some

images and think how quick the bridge was from
what was there to what was not, so quick a

bridge it flows, a river of bridges, making and
bursting, leaping and settling down, sidling

into pure extreme and middling back to its
other's mix: song's buoyance underlofts

anything and plays, sways it, puts it into play,
sheds the rigor of its stasis, makes forms wash

and even, playing, forms washes: anything,
anything, anything is poetry: effortlessness

keys the motion; it is a plentiful waste and
waste of plenty: no let up: there is a

maundering rover way up that like the jet stream
wanders down engaging its plenty with the

manifold, spraying energy into a million circuits
and circles, then playing through, regathering

and touching off again: this is awful, like
a descension of the gods, but, of course, there

are no gods but these, now, so it is not like
the gods, it is the gods: but I catch little

of the shine of such singings and prowlings; my
poetry is strawbags full of fleas the dogs won't

sleep on or rats rummage: I am the abstract inexact's
chickenfeed: I am borderlines splintered down

into hedgerows: I am the fernbrake ditches
winter brown, the shaggy down springs' flows

accrue: but think what it would be like to get
every word in, to trickle every rhythm in and

the overrhythms curling, lagging, eddying along
a network of motional obbligatos: imagine

getting all the elements in (including the
element of surprise), the axis each philodendron

leaf takes to the window, gathering it up round
and dumping it where it belongs in the sweeping,

the unheard, the unspent, that which is around
the edges of whatever may be: everything

assimilated to star-ypointing song: would that
not ease the mind, if discommode breakfast,

unhinge federal taxation): one reads of
travelers to the isles and continent and it's

castles, paintings, abbeys, cabs, and
callings-on (all that antedated western slop)

but who reports taking a leak or blithely oozing
a porch fart—well, it seems okay to mention

constipation (the higher morality) because
nobody ever goes, or can: when those bannered

armies assembled in the dawn to the earliest
clarions or meagerest quiet of the other camp,

had the respective parties already dookied in
the woods (something saved for battle): did

they do at the same places in the woods, a
centering constellation, or were there hills

from the top of which and down the sides of
which tumbled the goods to deep gatherings: we

are primates: apes: we're meat wrapped round
knotchbone spine: we can't untangle ourselves

productively from stalwart lacing, bone, artery,
nerve compact but, turned around, there is the

spiritual face, thoughts lightbeam light,
twinklings like minnows surfacing waves, the

rosy rushes that rouge or loft flesh, the
interface of meat and madness, love and lumbar:

it is, I think, remarkable that we are there in
the form of apes: mulling apes: walky apes:

but Newton, a lone one in his room, flowed
figure into calculus that found on a sheet of

paper the slow Saturn fell into passing Jupiter:
this kind of ape will join his fellows in a

dirty street and hack another fellow who has
done ungroupliness to death, axe him right

in the pleading face and let him bleed reconciled:
purity of cluster will override good or bad in

us: I have a low view of us: but that is why
I love us or try to move to love us: this

afternoon at the center downtown an old
violinist stood before 25 or 30 children, all

violinists, from 5 to, say, 11, and they played
together almost stilted sharp and classical: a

black child, all types of Asian, white—there
together, their bows striding in synch: the

mild trance in absented faces, the inner study
of outer music: a holiness, the same music

flowing through all of them, the all observing
the sway: I'm a goofball all right, one of

the hurt, one of the criers, one of the shaken
lovers: if love were likely it would not be

love: the ape squats to his business in the
woods and if a snake doesn't approach him

effluence of stars may ghostly appear fine-tuning
his nerves, daze him with dazzle magic: may

the gods or appetitive ganglions grant us,
mornings, the long grays, a run, a winding,

lane, trail, stone fence, narrative, coffee
shop, a will not to fall inward, slow, ease

still: a lively possibility like a rocky brook near
birches, a lean swerve, a trout's dorsal in

stone-water, a point, ever, of vigorous
answering, as with a click beetle, the rotary

narrowing by which a squirrel shucks a spruce
cone: not to fan out like a melt stream fading

into a valley, too thin a stream to cut its
gathering onward, not the blank wall backing a

shallow cave: preying, one thing or another,
and praying, one for another: sinister issues

The heap of knickknacks (knickknackatery),
whatnots (whatnotery), doodads, jews-harps,

belt buckles, do-funnies, files, disks, pads,
pesticide residues, nonprosodic high-tension

lines, whimpering-wimp dolls, epichlorohydrin
elastomotors, sulfur dioxide emissions, perfume

sprays, radioactive williwaws: the people at
Marine Shale are said to be "able to turn

wastes into safe products": but some say these
"products are themselves hazardous wastes":

well, what does anybody want: is there a world
with no bitter aftertaste or post coital triste:

what's a petit mort against a high moment:
I mean, have you ever heard of such a thing:

what about genetically engineered microorganisms
and a bright future: where's your faith, man:

try a little dirt, get a little tenderness: but
poetry is itself like an installation at Marine

Shale: it reaches down into the dead pit
and cool oil of stale recognition and words and

brings up hauls of stringy gook which it arrays
with light and strings with shiny syllables and

gets the mind back into vital relationship with
communication channels: but, of course, there

is some untransformed material, namely the poem
itself; the minute its transmutations end, it

becomes a relic sometimes only generations or
sets of countrywide generations can degrade:

a real stick in the fluencies: a leftover light
that hinders the light stream: poems themselves

processing, revitalizing so much dead material
become a dead-material concentrate time's

longest actions sometimes can't dissolve: not
to worry: the universe is expected to return

and the heat concentrate then will ashen wispy poetry
wispier: actually, the planet is going to

be fine, as soon as the people get off: and
why bother with carcinogenic residues—one

solar flare (nova) will recall all to light:
I'll tell you: I'm just not worried: in fact,

there is a saying that should be repeated in
piano interludes—don't worry, be happy: hold

that thought, it is life's best protection against
thought: when you can't put something out of

the world, put it out of your mind: but don't
just put something out of your mind—that leaves

a hole: put something you want to think about
in the hole and what that doesn't fill it will

displace: happiness is like anything else: if
you get it you ought to have to make it: that

is why happiness is, according to B. Googe, like
money, which one also has to make (or steal or

inherit): our society has made it clear it
doesn't much care how you get it: money is like

going to the cleaners, it comes back shiny,
spotless: why: because money is such an easy

(if you have it) access to power; it negotiates
instantly into desire and as it spends its way

into satisfaction it is desire itself desiring
itself: remember—don't sorry, be sappy: but

what money can't buy, celebrity can: celebrity
renders more of its past harmless than any other

agency: you can get up there where if you don't have
clay feet you ought to because otherwise you

impose on folks cruelly the burden of dealing with
your shining with no help from your screwups:

people above accusation's harm should have
something to be accused of: if my past erupts

before me, now, I'll pat it on the head and
have a milkbone with it: whimsies, gewgaws,

taradiddles, muffins, layer cakes, the time of
day to day: rains in the rainiest spring, with

six days to go, and sulfur-bright rings still
rim the puddles, so much pollen, the blue

spruce, its loft licked with cones: the right
time to write is when you have nothing to say,

your purview unrifted by the prejudice of personal
flows or ores, serenity which has balanced its

debits and credits annihilated, equanimity
circling without content or interruption:

beware the interests of the interested; theirs
might not include yours: take my word for it:

when you come to something not worth saying,
you might as well say so and say it: still, I

wish that in the interclustering of formations,
motions, ridge-swerves, upclimbings, and downward

ramifications, there were a preferential path, not
just a pathology of one, but a statistically

broad road announcing "the way"—or does
compensation work right out to the extremest

degree, the middle way nothing but nothing and
the broad road too wide to declare a narrowing:

words are crepe paper, skinny skeins, tissues of
misrepresentation: it doesn't matter if

they ding and dong, swirl up in ecstatic
windings: the true matter is without matter,

a sound nowhere head, just beyond tangible windows
and doors: but paint the husks feather-bright

because they wither! poetry is not logic or
knowledge or philosophy; it is action and

action's pleasure, but where does action end
and pleasure end, short of logic altogether,

not a dabble in theology, so airy and delightful:
you take even my old history teacher, his

commanding command of vocabulary was just part
of the trouble he couldn't stop talking, now

he's sitting in ward so and so, muttering: so,
put a period here and there, come around to a

closure, give somebody else the word: shut up
reticence's fullness in emptiness

should I go on, fearful of the phobias, strung
out, worried about the muttering asylums, working

the seams and veins of a fabric not designed to
be cut out as square as tapestry, seeking the

self-justifying inherences, the internal minglings
that might touch on a living center, and feeling

scared that the outer design is not predetermined
and probably not to be found, all these isolated

sketches and componencies not subordinated, as
the government of large tracts necessitates, to

a single effect, one graspable object having
outline and shape, the entire register of millions

of events made available to a single key or tone
or image, a collection, a region mapped, defined

and named—North Dakota: but the binding squeezes
of rightangling, rectilinear propagations move

in at times too tightly or living, winding,
exfoliating centers and trim the spirit too

sharply back: you can't classify except by
breaking down: some people say some things are

sacred and others secular and some say everything
is sacred or everything is secular: but if

everything is sacred (or secular), then what is
that: words, which attach to edges, cannot

represent wholeness, so if all is all, the it
just is: snakes have been worshipped, but I

consider them a little on the light side of
sacred, and although evil brown recluses electrify

dark corners with meaning, thus making cleanings
paradisiacal, I don't suppose they can quite

symbolize resurrection, the way scarabs can:
still, it seems evident that in the lush mercy

of the giver of things one should not be so
sparing as to think that generosity would trim

a slither off the divinity of any creature: so
it is all probably not a matter of the sacred

and secular, the good and bad, virtuous and
evil but a matter of measure; that is, it is

the fullness thereof; and all things that exist
are full of the fullness thereof and cannot,

without loss, be tapped, drained, squooshed, or
stuck on fine little pins: to be on the lookout

for evil (swamp rattlers) is a form of paying
attention, and to pay attention is to behold the

wonder, and the rights, of things, so just as
the fear of losing something (or someone) increases

its value enormously, so wariness of vipers and
other maelstroms of panic give us the brilliant

morning, the sun brittle on the hill-line before
it pops an arc-glob: there may be some husks,

chaff which the wind bloweth away, right on the
bottom of things, such as poison hulls or juices

from lethal vines, so with that division, I would
rather call everything else holy, you know, even

plowing a good way into garbage, taking that on
as having, perhaps, just served a sacred function

or, having passed through the cleansing of decay,
jut about to: for, you know, forms are never

permanent form, change the permanence, so
that one thing one day is something else another

day, and the energy that informs all forms just
breezes right through filth as clean as a whistle:

all this stuff here is illusory, you know, and
while it gives you bad dreams and wilding desires

and sometimes makes you spit up at night, it is
the very efflorescence of the fountain of shapes,

so while I might regard the digestive fire lit
at the top of the mound a purifying ritual, the

white smoke an incense, highrising as a wish,
aromatic as a blessing, I think I would not be

blasphemous, unless, of course, we as fallen
creatures should divide things up and strive to

be holy, not whole: things go round and
round and tie up a fullness which I call the

reality, the reality of the soup that includes
all chunks, and the reality is holy in my view,

if one may be permitted a view in matters so
significant: it is generally held by scientific

people and even some secular humanists that if
you visit immediate outer space you will not

find the protals of heaven but a metallic
clutterment you should be trying to go at the

same speed as: similar orbits, similar speeds:
time, space, and such like gets funny and you

could suffer a hit in the head by an overthrusted
tidbit: but it can seem slow, as with an

18,000½ mph object overtaking an 18,000 mph
object—it can seem to take all day, if there

were a day up there (there'll be no night): see
what I mean: days are little bent rectangles

turned round the world: actually, days are
durances in the eternal beam the diurnal earth turns

(daily?) through: but don't feel bad about the
celestial garbage, orbits thick and thin: it is

composed of the same matter that rusts in the
asteroids or fusions in the sun: celestial

garbage is so far the highest evidence of our
existence here: except for that vehicle that

got away: but the mystique of high places lingers
on, the altar-like flames residual in the high

levels of trash management: asteroids could pepper
earth to auras of salt-white pumice with the indifference

the collar of the launch missile could whack you
bumfuzzled: if there is to be any regard for

human life, it will have to be ours, right regard
for human life including all other forms of life,

including plant life. when we eat the body of
another animal, we must undergo the sacrifice

of noticing that life has been spent into our
life, and we must care, then, for the life we

have and for the life our life has cost, and we
must make proper acknowledgments and sway some

with reverence for the cruel and splendid tissue
biospheric: I love a poem every bit assimilated

into motion, whereas some will dwell with a
rubbish heap of bone, boulder, rust weir, wing

feather, cot spring, sounds pretty nice: properly
turned out, anything can most please me:

anxiety likes (an anxious person likes) to sit
midst an emptiness, emtiness wearing away, absorbing

the nettles and inflictive formations of things,
whereas cold folks love the stimulations of

pricks and tensions, intolerable griefs and
leanings, terrifying risks and exposures: the

cold out of all this terror at a pleasant move
only: can you imagine: even, though, the

anxious calm down occasionally and want to turn
away from the boredom of coming down and the

boredom of anxiety by taking an interest in
something: even, sometimes, taking a little

interest in something displaces the anxiety,
refocuses the attention, puts the mind off

itself: on a shelf is a good place to put the
mind: the mind, I have heard so much in its

praise: it comes to your rescue only if you've
already heard of it: the wise, though, have

all the time been gobbling, balling, iffing, fighting:
the mind's a pale savior: the soup it brings

is clearer even than the high recipes of
anxiety, the zombie land of totally present

totally absent: but it pacifies the losers,
it absorbs the distractions from the actual:

there is a place for it: anxiety can go into
Wanamaker's, for example, and breeze the aisles of

its way in burning networks throughout the nine
levels or so of merchandise and look for nothing,

stumble on nothing, nothing of interest: it
will, on the other hand, name the spot on a kid's

collar, think universal thoughts about some
artificial piece of defenestration or

look under the occult, religious, or children's
section for a nonexistent book of poems: out of

it: wow: patience wants to know how to needle
and thread and what oil to use on the threading

spool and why sometimes the best piece of
wood is not right for what you have in mind:

prosodically speaking, anxiety is none too keen
on entanglements, as with the bitchy requirements

of form or rhyme: being trapped into a failing
consideration, or simply being trapped, races

anxiety up a rev too high: anxiety wants to
now through: a clean sweep, forget the legislation

and, often, truly, it can be so nice to watch
the classical move through the complication, as

with Larry Bird en route for a lay-up, and
anxiety often itself has such heights of stalled

cumuli it can perform miracles, it can in seeking
ease deal with more substance than a clanking bore

can: it can, oh, yes, and that is the best
kind of poetry, the kind that seeking resolution

and an easing out of tension still out-tenses the
intensifiers: understatement rides swells

of easing away: anything else is sunk barges,
no gouging good, and practically everything

else is like that: the hackers, having none,
hack away at intensity: they want to move,

disturb, shock: they show the idleness of
pretended feeling: feeling moves by moving

into considerations of moving away: real
feeling assigns its weight gently to others,

helps them meet, deal with the harsh, brutal,
the ineluctable, eases the burdens of unclouded

facts: the strident hackers miss no chance to
dramatize, hurt, fairly or unfairly, for they

fear their emptiness: the gentlest, the most
refined language, so little engaged it is hardly

engaging, deserves to tell the deepest wishes,
roundabout fears: loud boys, the declaimers,

the deaf listen to them: to the whisperers,
even the silent, their moody abundance: the

poem that goes dumb holds tears: the line,
the fire line, where passion and control waver

for the field, that is a line so difficult to
keep in the right degree, one side not raiding

the other: if I reap the peripheries will I
get hardweed seed and dried roughage, roughage

like teasel and cattail and brush above snow in
winter, pure design lifeless in a painted hold.